Set Pieces

Set Pieces

BEING ABOUT FILM STILLS MOSTLY

DANIEL MEADOWS

First published in 1993 by the
British Film Institute
21 Stephen Street
London W1P 1PL

British Library Cataloguing in Publication Data
A catalogue record for this book is available
from the British Library.

ISBN 0-85170-389-5
ISBN 0-85170-390-9

Front cover photograph: The arrival of the
pioneering flight of 'Spirit of St Louis', from
Ken Russell's *The Mystery of Doctor Martinu*

Frontispiece: an out-take from a set of stills
shot for Tony Palmer's film portrait of
Hindemith (1990) made for London Weekend
Television's *South Bank Show* – showing Paul
Waggett, a Social Security Appeals Tribunal
clerk from Southport, as Christ crucified in a
scene shot at St Francis Xavier church,
Everton, Liverpool.

Design: Axis, Manchester
Typesetting and Artwork Production:
Cornerhouse, Manchester

Printed in Great Britain by
Garden House Press
Perivale, Middlesex

__in memoriam__

Ann Meadows 1917-89
Richard Gethin 1911-88

Silver ashes

My mother hated to be photographed. Even before she was crippled with multiple sclerosis, she hated it. She was never at ease when a camera was about and I never managed to take her picture; not satisfactorily anyway. As a young woman she had been a smasher – you have only to look at her wedding photograph – but she was possessed of a sensitive intelligence and she hated the way a photograph bottles you, freezes you in a frame. She was too colourful to be summed up in monochrome, and too three-dimensional to be summed up in two. She didn't want labelling.

Towards the end – chin on fist – it was all she could do to prop her head long enough to throw you a smile from her wheelchair. I kept trying for a picture but, whenever she saw my camera, she'd mutter, 'You beast!' and shame me into putting it away.

I have no pictures of my mother and no gravestone either. It was her wish that her remains should be cremated and the ashes scattered on a piece of her garden which separates the house from a neighbouring churchyard. It was a piece of ground she knew well – she had gazed at it from her chair every day for God knows how many years. We respected her wishes and, when we shook her silver ashes from the grey plastic bottle in which they had come from the crematorium, we hosed them into the soil. We didn't want them blowing away.

She was wrong about photography, though. You see, I don't believe we remember the bad pictures, not as much as we remember the good ones anyway. Listen: I bet most of you can conjure up an image of Greta Garbo, mmm? A Hollywood still by Clarence Bull or one of Cecil Beaton's pictures perhaps – probably you won't know who took it – but I bet she looks gorgeous. And I bet it isn't one of those snapped towards the end of her life by a paparazzo, one which shows her in the distance, hiding from the camera, disguised in men's clothes. Of course it isn't! Garbo was a great beauty and that is how we choose to remember her.

Photographs, like gravestones, provide a focus for memory but, in the absence of either, I am compelled to create an alternative. The love of theatre which my mother passed to me from an early age is treasure indeed. In that, and so in the pages of this book, she lives on. Oh, those silver ashes!

Contents

Acknowledgments

With the exception of the frames of footage cut from Christine Edzard's *The Fool* (Sands Films © 1990) and reproduced on p.15, all photographs in this book are by Daniel Meadows and are copyright protected.

Photographs on the following pages are reproduced by courtesy of:

pp. 17, 19, 51, 55, 87 and back cover: London Trust Cultural Productions/RM Associates

frontispiece and pp. 57, 61, 63, 88, 89, 92, 93, 97: Isolde Films/RM Associates

pp. 13, 15, 21, 47, 49, 69, 70, 71, 72, 73, 74, 75, 103, 105, 107, 109, 115, 116: © Sands Films Ltd

p. 39: The Moving Picture Company

p. 113: Aurum Press Ltd/Express Newspapers plc

pp. 43, 45, 79: Dreamgrange Ltd/RM Associates

… to whom many thanks.

The pictures of Julian Bream on pp. 81, 83 and 85 were first published by Macdonald and Co (Publishers) Ltd in 1982

Otherwise all material is © Daniel Meadows

'Stand by to go, everyone! Red light and bell!
We're just waiting for the big brute in the sky'
First Assistant Director

You should know what you're looking at

I have called this book *Set Pieces* because I made nearly all the photographs in it whilst on assignment and most of my assignments these days seem to be on film sets. I do not earn my living exclusively from the film industry and I have never yet worked in Hollywood. However, since 1981, I have worked as unit stillsman on fifteen British-made films and I have found the experience fascinating and one I would like to share. I do not know whether my working method differs greatly from that of the other stillsmen I admire, like David Appleby or Murray Close, since I have never seen them working, but I cannot believe that what I do is *so* different that it limits the value of what I say.

A good many of the photographs in this collection have never been in print, some are 'out-takes' – 'kills' as they are known in the movie business – which I have plucked from files where they have lain forgotten ever since being rejected by some unit publicist or other. Some were shot even though I knew they would never be selected for the 'approved' set of stills; it was just that at the time I simply could not *resist* making them, like the frontispiece which amuses me because of the relationship between the actor playing Christ and the gas fire which has been wheeled up to keep him warm. Such pictures – pictures which draw on a photographer's observational skills – always delight me even though I know that there are plenty of cynics out there who will assume that the situation did not simply 'come about' but that the photographer in some way 'set it up'.

Today such cynicism is commonplace, for we live in the age of the digitised pixel and the computerised imaging device, retouching tools of such sophistication that seamless artifice is, all too often, the order of the day. When even that holiest of all shrines to man's determination to record in pictures that which occurs naturally – the *National Geographic* magazine[1] – owns up to electronically 'pushing together' two ancient pyramids in order to fit them onto its cover, who can blame *anyone* for doubting what they see in pictures?

More than ever, it is important that we know what we are looking at. In my case you simply have to take it on trust: when I looked through the camera and pressed the shutter, believe me, the picture I made is what you now see.

A neat slice of time

I make no claims for these pictures as 'art'. To me a photograph is a photograph and that's the beginning and end of it, 'a neat slice of time' as Susan Sontag so aptly puts it. 'Photographs,' she writes, 'may be more memorable than moving images, because they are a neat slice of time, not a flow.' I like that. 'Each still photograph is a privileged moment,' she says, 'turned into a slim object that one can keep and look at again.'[2]

And there's something else, another reason for doing this book. Since 1981 I have worked as a teacher of photography, a college lecturer, and it is in the spirit of a teacher, in the hope that budding photographers and film-makers everywhere might glean something useful – something that will at least save them embarrassment when they find themselves working on a film set for the first time – that I offer this work. Teaching and working in the movies both happened for me at the same time. So while working on documentaries and dramas, TV series like *Inspector Morse* (1988) as well as full-blown cinema features, I have also had several hundred students pass through my hands.

Tony Palmer, Christine Edzard and Ken Russell are the directors for whom I have worked most frequently and the pictures which appear in this book are for the most part selected from the stills shot on one or other of the following films. For Tony Palmer: *Death in Venice* (1981), a 16mm version of the Benjamin Britten opera; *Wagner* (1983), a 35mm nine-hour mini-series starring Richard Burton and Vanessa Redgrave; *Mozart in Japan* (1987), a documentary about the pianist Mitsuko Uchida; *Testimony* (1987), a wide-screen feature about the life of Dmitri Shostakovich, starring Ben Kingsley; *Hindemith* (1990), for London Weekend Television's *South Bank Show*; and *A Family Life* (1990), a documentary about Yehudi Menuhin. For Christine Edzard: *Little Dorrit* (1985), a 35mm six-hour two-part version of the Dickens novel starring Alec Guinness and with a cast of 250; *The Fool* (1991), a 35mm feature starring Derek Jacobi and a with a cast of 181; and *As You Like It* (1992), a 35mm Shakespeare film with James Fox, Emma Croft and Griff Rhys Jones. For Ken Russell: *The Mystery of Doctor Martinu* (1992), a 16mm TV psychoanalysis of the Czech composer's dreams.

What are stills?

Stills are the photographs shot by the unit stillsman. They should, as near as possible, duplicate the imagery on the footage shot by the movie camera. The object is to show who is in the movie and what it looks like, to give - as the producers say - some indication of the movie's 'PV', its production value. 'Have we got some big names?' 'Yes.' 'Have we got beautiful women?' 'Yes.' 'Have we got wonderful scenery?' 'Yes.' 'Have we got steam trains?' 'Yes.' 'Have we got a car chase?' 'Yes.' 'Does it look like we've spent a whole lot of money on this picture?' 'Yes!' 'Well, then, let's see it in the goddamn stills!'

Some stills are in black and white and some are in colour. For reasons to do with the physical and chemical make-up of photographic emulsions, as well as the need to distribute the results in large numbers, the best quality black and white stills come as prints and the best quality colour stills come as transparencies (slides). The stillsman must shoot both.

Traditionally the stillsman shoots still photographs of every set-up shot during the making of a movie. At the end of each set-up the movie camera is rolled away, the stillsman steps into its place and the First Assistant Director instructs the actors (or 'artistes' as they are known in the movie business) to 'do it one more time from the top, just for stills'.

At least that's what *should* happen. On the average cinema feature a stills photographer is required to assemble a portfolio of about a hundred colour transparencies and fifty black and white prints from the many thousands of frames he will have put through his cameras during the making of the film. He will not be the final arbiter - indeed he may not be consulted at all over which stills are chosen. The producer, the director and the publicist, however, will all want their say.

The stillsman's pictures have four main functions:

1. To show financiers where their money has gone.
2. To help drum up enthusiasm for the movie among the world's film distribution companies.
3. To promote the film in magazine features, newspaper previews and reviews, on posters and on merchandise.
4. For display in those glazed cabinets outside the cinema.

Photograph 1
Irina Brook in *The Fool*

Why can't producers snip stills from *their* footage?

Well, sometimes they do … but not if the publicity people have anything to do with it because, more often than not, magazine picture editors reject prints or transparencies made in this way as being too blurred, too 'grainy'. Blur is caused by the movie camera operating at a shutter speed of 1/50 second, which is not always fast enough to freeze movement. Grain is the random dot pattern from which the photographic image is formed.

The picture on the cinema screen doesn't *appear* blurred or grainy because 24 separate frames of it – each one moving the action on, each one with its own individual grain pattern – pass through the projector every second. You don't see the grain because it changes from frame to frame, but cut out one of those frames and print it up, and it looks like a pointillist painting viewed through the bottom of a beer glass. Or, as we photographers say: 'It'll have grain like golf balls.'

So why aren't the *stills* blurred? Both movie and still images are made on the same size (35mm) film, aren't they? And it's all the same photographic process, isn't it?

Well, yes, except for two things:

1. The stillsman is not restricted to 1/50 second. Even in quite low light levels he can use faster shutter speeds to freeze the action.
2. Where in a movie camera the long side of the rectangular frame of the image runs *across* the film, in a still camera it runs *along* the film. Thus the picture made in a 35mm still camera is more than twice the size of its equivalent in a 35mm movie camera. There is no doubt about it: the stillsman's stills have the edge when it comes to quality.

One more thing. The movie you see in the cinema is a first-generation print from a negative created in the movie camera. The movie's negative is precious and easily damaged; it represents the entire investment of the film's makers (as much as $70m these days). It is stored in a lab and handled only by trained technicians, who do not take kindly to publicists helping themselves to it to make endless dupes for distribution to magazines.

So, inconvenient though it is to have yet another person cluttering up his film set, the film producer has little choice but to employ a stillsman to shoot his stills for him.

Photograph 2
35mm footage: from the still camera (left) and from the movie camera (right). Picture: the Shillibeer party in *The Fool*.

Silver dreams

I can't say exactly when it was that I first became interested in the cinema, though I can remember the first film I ever went to: it was Disney's *Snow White and the Seven Dwarfs* (1937). I saw it as a small boy at the Regal Cinema in Cheltenham sometime in the 1950s. We didn't have a television at the time so the whole language of moving pictures was totally new to me. I remember how frightened I was of the wicked witch – her face, twelve feet high, filling my field of vision – and she visited my nightmares with that apple, oh! for years and years.

I *can* say exactly when it was that I decided I wanted to be a photographer: it was when I was seventeen during a film club screening of Antonioni's *Blow Up* (1966).

If I'm really honest, though, the most wonderful thing about that film was not so much David Hemmings being a photographer as Vanessa Redgrave being Vanessa Redgrave.

I had first seen her in a movie I have subsequently seen many times and still enjoy – Karel Reisz's *Morgan, A Suitable Case for Treatment* (also 1966) – but it was in *Blow Up* that I fell in love with her. Thirteen years were to pass before I finally got to photograph her in the flesh (it was on the set of Tony Palmer's *Wagner* in Venice in 1982), and such was my infatuation I could barely hold the camera steady. Since then I have tried to adopt a more professional approach.

I have never been a movie 'train-spotter', not like all those people you meet on film sets who can tell you every film this or that actor was ever in. What I do like about films, though, is the acting – that peculiar thing indulged in by grown-ups who dress up and pretend to be altogether other people and in the process make you laugh and make you cry. That's the magic of the cinema for me. And, as a photographer, it is more fun to photograph them doing it on a film set where they are lit for photography and where you can chat to them between 'takes', than in the theatre where photographers are herded into the pit and allowed to take their pictures only from a distance during something called a 'photocall'.

Going to the theatre, though, is something my family always did. As a child it was one of the great delights of school holidays.

Photograph 3
Vanessa Redgrave, Venice

Actor knights

My mother kept the programmes of all the post-war theatre performances she attended. I have these programmes now and, looking through them, I see the names and photographs of many actors I have subsequently photographed – John Gielgud, Ralph Richardson, Laurence Olivier, Ben Kingsley, Peggy Ashcroft; and many more whom I wish I had photographed but now never will – Michael Redgrave, Joyce Grenfell, Anthony Quayle, Sybil Thorndyke, Jack Hulbert, Paul Robeson.

From the age of eight I began to join my parents on their trips to the theatre. I can't remember everything they took me to see but some Stratford performances are indelible: Janet Suzman in *Taming of the Shrew*, Paul Scofield in *Macbeth* (both 1967), Judy Dench in *Twelfth Night* (1969) … John Gielgud was my mother's favourite and when, in early 1982, I went to Vienna to photograph him on the set of Tony Palmer's *Wagner*, she was most curious to know what he was 'like'.

It was an important moment in movie history: the only occasion when the 'three old boys' (as they were known to the *Wagner* crew) had appeared together in the same scene of a film. The photograph which was used to promote the film – and the one which appears in the biographies of both Richardson and Olivier – was not the picture opposite but a close-up of their three heads. I prefer this picture, though, because it shows them all standing to their marks. See, on the floor, the camera tape put there by the loader. Three actor knights all toeing the line.

I had tonsillitis and a temperature of 101°F at the time, and I remember I had but a few seconds to shoot my pictures (not that there was anything strange about that). Standing alongside me was a local stills photographer whom I had been brought out to replace. What happened to *his* pictures I don't know and what happened to the colour ones I took I don't know either, except that they are lost. A photograph is a fragile thing.

Sadly, and much to her disappointment, I had to tell my mother what I tell everyone who asks me what an actor is 'like' – that I don't know. When *I* photograph actors they are always pretending to be someone else! In this case Gielgud was being Pfistermeister, an official at the court of mad King Ludwig of Bavaria.

Photograph 4
Ralph Richardson, Laurence Olivier and John Gielgud on the set of *Wagner* in Vienna

A comedy of manners

Friends – photographers who work on their own ideas, researching, organising, shooting, editing, raising finance and selling finished stories for publication (as indeed I do myself when I'm not teaching or working in the film business) – often express surprise that I can take any pleasure at all from shooting pictures which are, after all, merely segments of someone else's concept, someone else's performance, someone else's lighting and someone else's directorial skill. 'Where is the satisfaction in it?' they ask. Where indeed? They are right, of course. Hanging about on the fringes of someone else's picture is not an obvious way for a photographer to pursue his career. I can only tell you the reasons why I keep going back for more.

The first reason I like shooting stills is that I get paid to see – and at very close quarters, closer even than if I had the best seat in the house were the thing being done in a theatre – a good many very high-calibre performances; and, because it is rare even for great actors to get it right on the first 'take' (and if they do you can be sure the director or the camera operator or the sound engineer or *someone* will find good reason for making them 'go again'), I am guaranteed at least one, and often several more, repeat performances. The snail's pace of film-making can be infuriating but, I find, the tedium of all the waiting around is more than counterbalanced by the sheer delight of witnessing a performance slowly build right in front of my eyes.

All right, call me a groupie and yes, perhaps there is something perverse in taking pleasure from the live aspects of a performance created especially for the screen, but there you go.

The second joy of shooting stills is something I find more difficult to explain. All I can say is that there is a unique sense of satisfaction to be had simply from *the doing of it*.

What a stills photographer has to do – shoot in black and white and in colour perfectly exposed stills to match the picture being created in the movie camera – is not quite as easy as it sounds. It *should* be easy but it isn't. Often it is almost impossible. There's a comedy of manners which surrounds the work of the stillsman and, like being able to distinguish between Marmite and chocolate spread, there's much misery to be had from getting it wrong – and vice versa.

Photograph 5
Griff Rhys Jones in *As You Like It*

Beginnings

Engineers of the imagination

But I didn't start in the business by photographing actor knights. My first theatrical commissions, back in the mid-70s, were done for a pittance and on assignment for 'alternative' theatre and theatre-in-education companies. At that time, the only way I could make anything over and above a minimal day rate was if I could sell my pictures to the actors or get them published in the newspapers. I became interested in the film business only when someone explained to me that the amount of money spent on the promotion and distribution of a movie is often half as much again as the amount spent on making the movie itself. It seemed that I'd stand a better chance of making a living in films.

But my theatre days were fun. My favourite clients were a group of performers who lived in caravans on a disused rubbish tip in Burnley and called themselves Welfare State International. (Based in Cumbria now, they are still going strong.) At the time they were creating quite a reputation for making energetic and anarchic street theatre in which they always tried to involve the local people. Their work never failed to entertain and, whenever possible, they created their costumes, props, songs, words, music, pyrotechnics and earthworks anew for every show. They mixed the spectacular and the grotesque with an engaging strain of playfulness and no occasion brought to their attention, however small, was considered unworthy of celebration.

The biggest gig I photographed for them was their 'Parliament in Flames' show on 5 November 1976 when 10,000 people turned out to process through the town and witness the burning down of a huge replica of the Houses of Parliament. A 30ft high Guy was lowered onto the flames from a 100ft crane and the sky was lit up for miles around.

The smallest gig I photographed for them was a naming ceremony (opposite) which took place in and around a cave near Ingleborough. The man presiding is Boris Howarth and, like all good actors, his reputation preceded him. I had been warned about Boris. Word was that you had to avoid going out for a drink if Boris was in the vicinity, for he had once turned up unannounced at a quiet rural pub dressed in a costume made almost entirely out of lampshades and had spoiled the locals' drinking habits of a lifetime by proceeding to stab stuffed birds on the piano.

Photograph 6
New Year's Day 1978. By the light of burning torches a snip of hair was cut from each child's head and buried in the earth on the floor of a massive cave. The children made boats from twigs and sailed them in a stream which ran through the cave. Afterwards there was a party and pigeons were released.

Civic magicians

Here he is again.

The first time I saw Boris perform was in Birmingham. In a parody of posh theatre, Welfare State had taken over a building site (where now the city library stands) right in the city centre. Half buried in the ground between two unfinished multi-storey buildings was (as I remember) a collection of seven motorcars. They were painted brown and dusted with fuller's earth. Around them, in paper holders, a circle of candles was lit. The audience watched from the jutting floors of unfinished buildings – a sort of undressed dress circle, if you like – which afforded a fine view; and, as darkness fell, a string quartet, perched high in the architecture and picked out by a spotlight, struck up a discordant and haunting tune. A singer joined in, shrilly wailing: 'I am a child of the city, I am a child of the city…' on and on.

At breakneck speed and with a great to-do, a military-style winch truck (of the kind used to pull tanks out of the mud) roared into the arena knocking over candles and smashing into the cars. It was driven by robots in black town-planner suits, and, in a specially constructed light tent attached to the back of it, a dancer performed a shadow dance. As the truck came to a halt the robots jumped out, dug up the end of a wire hawser planted in the ground, and attached it to the winch. With much revving of the engine, the winch began its work. For a while nothing happened. Then, with a screech, the cars quite literally jumped into the air. It was a resurrection. As Boris later told me: 'We had literally driven them into the ground, and now we were bringing them to life again.'

Then, with the singer still wailing 'I am a child of the city, I am a child of the city!' there began from out of the depths of what had now become a kinetic sculpture a low moaning sound as, one against the other, the cars scraped together, metal on metal. As if someone was slowly turning up the volume the moan gradually grew into a great scream which drowned all the other noises of the city night, even the applause of the audience.

It was fantastic.

What it meant I haven't a clue, but I know I'll never forget it.

When they began paying me for photographing their gigs, their cheques drew on a bank account named 'Galactic Smallholdings'.

Photograph 7
From *The Loves, Lives and Trials of Lancelot Icarus Handyman Barabbas Quail* (1977), a demon figure with a folded paper collar, insulating tape ears and wired coat

Pathological optimists

Welfare State's performances were derived from the nomadic English Theatre of the sixteenth century. Their work is well documented in the book *Engineers of the Imagination* by Tony Coult and Baz Kershaw (Methuen, 1983). I have never come away from one of their shows without feeling that once again life is good and that the world is a very fine place to be.

When I look back on those gigs, I realise that working with Welfare State – the hum of generators, the hard work, the smoke, the unit catering, the caravans, the heightened sense of occasion, the tension, the costumes, the mud, the cold, the endless cups of coffee, the dependence upon the weather, the sheer scale of the operation and the exhilaration when it all went well – was so similar to the experience of working on a movie location that it is really no wonder that, in due course, I began to gravitate towards working in films.

Before I worked on the big screen, though, I went to work on the small one.

I remember once, when I was photographing a street pageant Welfare State had organised in Ulverston, I saw a crowd of people staring into a shop window, their backs to the procession. When I broke off to see what could possibly be more absorbing than the live show going on in the street, I saw that they were watching television: Wimbledon it was, McEnroe and Borg slogging their way through a nail-biting tie-break in the fourth set.

Ah, the pull of the telly!

By 1978 I had ten theatre companies on my books including the Northern Ballet Theatre, the Bolton Octagon Theatre and Manchester University's Contact Theatre. In between journalistic and other, self-originated, assignments I was producing front-of-house and publicity pictures but still I was only just about managing to get by. Then a picture story I had done about a psychiatric hospital, published in the *Observer Magazine*, led to my being offered a job as a programme researcher at Granada TV in Manchester.

It was an offer I couldn't refuse. My days as a theatre photographer were over. With some misgivings I hung up my cameras and joined the 'meedja'.

Photograph 8
Borg vs McEnroe, 1980:
tie-break in the fourth set

A trip through the 'meedja'

Television

Granada must have been unique in taking chances with untested newcomers like me. I certainly had a lot to learn. I'd had doubts about joining television, not just because I had never worked in a big institution before, but because I found it a difficult medium to take seriously. I have always believed that, when reporting, the authority of what you say comes out of the intimacy you have with your subject, and what worried me about so much of what I saw on television, particularly on local television, was that its reporters seemed woefully out of touch with what was going on out on the streets and irredeemably keen to ape the networked style. So much of what one saw was obsessed with celebrity or sensation – fire, explosion, robbery, murder and motor accident – I wasn't sure how I would fit in.

But it was a wonderful opportunity to get some experience of making films and I had no intention of wasting it. They threw me in the deep end, making three-minute items for the local evening magazine programme. There was no training. I was expected to pick it all up as I went along, and it was tremendously exciting.

We worked exclusively with 16mm film (portable video came later), using the confusingly titled 'two plus two' crew. It was confusing because two plus two added up not to four crew members but ten. The four were the cameraman and his assistant and the sound man and his assistant. The others were the reporter, the director, two electricians, the researcher and the production assistant.

Small wonder the reporting lacked intimacy! It wasn't *necessary* to have so many people in the crew, not if film-making was the principal concern, but that's how it was done. The TV unions were very powerful at the time and film reporting was a cumbersome process. I well remember once having to interview a deaf old man about the condition of his gas fire (there had been an explosion). In order to accommodate everyone who needed to be in his tiny kitchen to film him, I had to perch myself on the draining board across the other side of the room.

'Camera rolling,' barked the director. 'Cue Daniel!'

'When was it that the gas board cut you off?' I shouted.

My subject cupped his hand to his ear: 'You what, lad?'

Photograph 9
In 1979 Margi Clarke, later to star in *Letter to Brezhnev* (1985), was known as 'Margox'. She presented a regional show called *What's On* for Granada TV.

Two plus two equals ten

Because a 'two plus two' crew cost about £1,000 a day to operate you could use it only sparingly. There was no time for little luxuries like familiarising your subjects with what the filming process entailed, giving them enough time to relax and appear 'natural'.

I found it all terribly frustrating.

I wanted very much to infuse my television reporting with the kind of subject rapport I had enjoyed as a photographer. The only way I could think of proceeding was to do away with the reporter's dependence on his camera crew and make reports using sequences of still pictures. These I enlarged and mounted on card which I then took to the location and presented as inserts to my reports or, as the jargon has it, my 'pieces-to-camera'. I was, in effect, making magazine picture stories for television.

Colleagues considered me eccentric for wanting to make, for a medium designed to show moving pictures, reports that used so many still ones, but – if for no other reason than that it looked like being cheap – my bosses encouraged me. My pilot film told the story of an industrial boiler fluer from Nelson, Lancashire, whose firm had recently gone out of business. He had been introduced to me as a man who lived out the punishment given to the serpent in the garden of Eden: 'Upon thy belly shalt thou go and eat dust all the days of thy life.' I shot stills of him crawling about in the dust of a factory's flues and presented my report from the hulk of a disused boiler in a Burnley scrapper's yard.

To my great joy the film met with approval and I was quickly commissioned to make more. I had 'arrived' or at least so I thought …

Then one morning, I came to work to find that my own trade union – whose rules restricted reporters to reporting and photographers to taking photographs – had blacked me. 'You're doing the work of two people,' my father of chapel told me. 'Photographers are in the ACTT, reporters are in NUJ.'

None of my reports was transmitted.

Restrictive practice was the order of the day. At times it was petty beyond belief. I recall a props man warning me against holding a chair for a studio guest. It was not my job to move the furniture, he said, and he wasn't joking.

Photograph 10
Margi Clarke, with son Lawrence on her knee, watches playback from studio

Blacked

Because of restrictive practices a lot of the people employed in television did not have much to do and I joined their ranks. For a time I shared a desk with a man who spent most of his days organising a complicated love life over the telephone and doing the *Guardian* crossword. He would come in at about ten o'clock in the morning and photocopy the crossword from the office newspaper. Then he would start phoning. It was some months before I realised that another colleague whose desk was but a few yards away, though on the other side of a partition, also spent his morning with the *Guardian* crossword, but he wasn't *completing* the crossword, he was *composing* it. Somehow I could never bring myself to reveal this discovery to my companion, perhaps because I was frightened it would destroy the delicate balance of his life.

The balance of my own life was shaken up at this time because I got married. I remember returning to my desk after my honeymoon to be greeted cheerfully by the crossword ladies' man with: 'Now tell me, what's your first wife called?' Working in television threatened to make cynics of us all.

Some wag said at the time: 'Television is a medium because it's neither rare nor well done.' He was right.

My last days at Granada were spent in a rehearsal room playing games of the custard-pie and ferret-down-the-trousers kind commissioned from a lady poet who needed the work. It was my job to try these games out to see if they were suitable for an afternoon show in which members of the public pitted their embarrassment thresholds against those of various celebrities.

In the evenings I amused myself by shooting pictures for Manchester's music guru and fellow Granada employee, Tony Wilson. Wilson had just completed two successful series of the popular music programme *So It Goes* and, in his spare time, ran a record company called Factory which was then enjoying its first success with the band Joy Division.[3] Wilson's instructions were that I shoot blurred pictures, and lots of them, of the lead singer Ian Curtis. Here is one of them (opposite). A few months later Curtis committed suicide and the band broke up, only to re-form under the name New Order. I didn't have any orders but I could feel my life slipping away.

It was time to be off.

Photograph 11
Ian Curtis, singer with Joy Division

Beauty from ashes

I went back to freelancing for newspapers and magazines. But I was no newsman. I was a dad, with a young son whom I rarely saw because work was always taking me away. Freelancing for newspapers is no kind of life for a family man. No fun to make the news and, as a friend of mine discovered in no uncertain measure, no fun to be in it either.

He was a priest, a fat priest. His family owned a chain of cinemas and he had been expected to follow his father into the business. If your dad's in pictures you don't need a lucky break. He would have become a film editor if he hadn't had The Call.

He is a real 'life enhancer', my pal the priest, not a pie-in-the-sky-when-you-die type at all. In pictures he would have made Cecil B. DeMille look to his laurels, let me tell you. He certainly knew how to make them jump. Back in the 70s he started a housing association for the single homeless and one-parent families and, whether they know it or not, today more than two thousand people owe him the roof over their heads. He didn't make shorts, my pal, he worked in epics.

He used to pop in unannounced to talk about the films. He wanted to know about Deborah Kerr in *The Assam Garden*, and when the picture came to town he got up a party to go and see it. And he was greatly moved by a colour still I did of the DHSS tribunal clerk who played Christ crucified in Tony Palmer's *Hindemith*. Now, of course, I wish I'd given him a print of it.

He was undone when a story about him broke in a Sunday paper. GAY SEX SCANDAL, PRIEST QUITS JOB ran the banner headline in our local rag. There were no charges, there was no hearing, just the inky finger of Fleet Street. Afterwards the mother of the bride whose delayed wedding had had to be performed by a stand-in while my pal made his escape said: 'I thought it was odd that the other side had so many photographers.'

I don't hear from him any more. They say he's in America, in a Catholic funny farm, but I don't know.

I bet he wishes he *had* gone into pictures. In church the only prayers they say for him are silent ones. This sinner sends one up now and again. Isaiah 61:3: 'The Lord has anointed me to make beauty from ashes.' If anyone put out The Call for me, I didn't hear it. I went into movies.

Photograph 12
Deborah Kerr hitches a lift. In *The Assam Garden*, during a long crane shot, Miss Kerr had to walk along a path into some trees and emerge in the distance as the camera rose high to take in the wider view. But in the trees, and out of sight from the camera position, there was a pond. Two riggers were quickly volunteered to carry Miss Kerr around the pond at the double. Director Mary McMurray gives chase while Madhur Jaffrey reads.

Some technical bits

The film crew

The first time I worked on a film set, I couldn't believe that five people are employed to operate the camera … five people to do with the movie equipment what a stillsman has to do all by himself! There's a man to load the film stock and operate the clapper board (the clapper loader); a man to maintain the equipment, to measure the focus with a tape measure and to operate the stop (the focus puller); a man to frame the shot and to pan and tilt the camera (the operator), and a man to light the set (the director of photography). There is also someone (key grip) to control the movement of the camera on its wheels (the dolly).

The stillsman works right alongside the movie camera; all these people must be his friends, he needs them. If he rubs them up the wrong way they can make his job impossible.

Once, during a long take, I turned round and counted the number of people on the set behind the camera. There were over eighty of them: assistant directors, make-up artists, wardrobe assistants, propsmen, production assistants, electricians (gaffer, best boy and sparks), chippies, drivers, painters, riggers, extras, the list goes on … But the thing the stillsman has to remember is that all these people have one thing in common: they are there to make the job of acting easier.

The stillsman is the only member of the crew whose work makes no contribution whatever to easing the actors' lot. Many actors object to being photographed while they are working and it is very easy for a pushy stillsman to find his job made extremely difficult. Every photographer develops his own style of working: mine is to hang back, to blend in and to push myself forward only when it is absolutely vital. It was a style I adopted on my very first day working for a film director and, because it has served me well, I've stuck with it.

That job was for Tony Palmer, who hired me to photograph an orchestra recording a movie soundtrack. ('Absolutely no clicks during the take!') Unknown to me Palmer had – the day before – hired another photographer (a woman) to do the same job and, when the session was over, he asked the orchestra what they thought of the photographer. None of them could remember a man taking pictures, only the woman … so I was hired for the movie.

Photograph 13
Hannah King stands on 'paganinis' (wooden blocks) to embrace Patrick Ryecart in Ken Russell's *The Mystery of Doctor Martinu*, while crew members shield her from the wind and the public gaze.

Taking off

Following my experiences of restrictive practices in television, I was wary of entering the film business because I had heard that in movies things were, if anything, even worse. Magnum[4] photographer David Hurn (of whom more later) told me a story which illustrates only too well just how bad things used to be.

Baking on the runway in the North African desert, a film unit – consisting of a hundred or so individuals (of whom he was one) all with first-class travel written into their contracts of employment – was boarding a plane to move to its next location. The first-class cabin, in the rear of the plane, soon filled up but the economy class, at the front of the plane, remained empty. Over the tannoy the captain asked if some of the first-class passengers (all film people) would mind moving forward because the plane could not take off unless their weight was more evenly dispersed. No one moved. Too many people stood to lose too much face by flying economy class. It took, apparently, several hours of fierce negotiation in the intense noonday sun before reason eventually prevailed and the plane was able to fly.

As it happens, by the time I went into films, things had relaxed considerably. The British film industry has been a twitching carcass for so long that the people working in it – moguls and technicians alike – do seem to have concluded that the only way they can eke a living from it is if everyone is a little more tolerant and a little less suspicious of each other's motives. With as few as fifty British film dramas being made each year – and most of those for TV and on low budgets – the industry's future hangs in the balance.

A recent estimate suggests that, for every film crew member currently in work, five are sitting at home twiddling their thumbs or using the family runabout to provide a local minicab service. Now that all the big studios have gone 'four wall' (that is, sacked their full-time staff) the heart has gone out of the film industry. There are, for instance, no longer any young apprentices being trained to take the place of the older technicians. One camera operator I know gets by during his time out by making false teeth for sheep. Twenty years ago he'd have been showing trainees how to use a lathe or take a camera to pieces.

Who are the stills photographers?

Apart from the unit stills there are two other kinds of photograph shot on a film set: continuity stills and special assignment stills.

Continuity stills are shot as an *aide-mémoire* for the props men, the art director, the wardrobe assistants, the make-up artists and everyone else who needs to remember where anything should go. How was this tie done up? How many buttons were undone? How full was that glass of wine? What was the time on the clock? What colour jumper was she wearing when we did the other half of this shot six weeks ago?

These days, anyway since the invention of the Polaroid camera, most of these people shoot their own continuity stills and it is no longer common to find a photographer assigned exclusively to the job. But it's an important job. For instance, in the big party scenes on *Little Dorrit* and *The Fool* – a nightmare for continuity, with actors in elaborate Victorian costumes eating and drinking, dancing and constantly circulating – I remember the wardrobe department had, in addition to several ring binders full of ten by eight inch black and white continuity stills, a whole series of detailed drawings pinned to the studio wall showing how each male artiste's necktie should be tied and how the ladies should wear their jewellery.

The continuity still is a humble thing, but not to be underestimated.

The Special Assignment Photographer, on the other hand, is a big cheese sent from a big-circulation magazine or hired specially by the film company in the hope that his byline or hers (American photographer Annie Leibovitz is among the best 'specials' working today) will be sufficient to guarantee the film big spreads of pictures in the world's leading magazines. On two of the films I did for Christine Edzard, Lord Snowdon was special assignment photographer. He worked four days on *Little Dorrit* (for *Liberation* in France and the *Sunday Times Magazine* in the UK) and two days on *The Fool* (for the *Telegraph Magazine*).

During a film's run, its publicist also tries to secure deals for the exclusive publication of the 'special' stills with one or other of the principal magazines in the next country where the film is due to open. The other magazines, newspapers, listings journals and the like have to make do with the unit stillsman's pictures.

Photograph 15
Lord Snowdon

The special assignment photographer

Unlike the unit stillsman, the 'special' does not necessarily shoot pictures which look like the footage. Magazine editors are reluctant to give over their feature pages to articles which seem to do little more than provide free advertising for a new movie, and consequently they are resistant to showing too many pictures of what a film actually looks like. Also, being obsessed with personalities, they like to grace their pages with 'yummy' lit colour portraits of the stars. The way Snowdon's pictures taken on *Little Dorrit* were used is a good example of this.

Lord Snowdon did not work on the set shooting action footage, he shot studio portraits. A space was created away from the set which he lit with a giant diffuser containing three enormous flash heads. He then shot a whole series of colour *carte de visite*-style formal photographs of all the principal actors – Sarah Pickering, Derek Jacobi, Alec Guinness, Cyril Cusack, Max Wall, Joan Greenwood, Eleanor Bron, Roshan Seth, Michael Elphick, Patricia Hayes and the rest – and it was these that were used in magazine exclusives, sometimes on their own and sometimes supported by one or two of the unit stills.

Another example of the difference between the work of the unit stillsman and the 'special' can be seen in Penguin Books' special film edition of *Little Dorrit* (1986). On the cover there is a full-page colour photograph taken through a wet windowpane of Little Dorrit walking in the Marshalsea prison yard. (This picture was also used for the film's poster.) Printed over it in white capital letters are the words 'Colour photographs by Lord Snowdon'. As it happens, this picture is mine. I tell you this not out of any sense of injustice – I am credited for the picture in the usual way on the back cover – but the publishers obviously felt that Snowdon's name on the front cover along with twenty-four of his studio portraits printed inside, would assist the sales of the book.

Snowdon has done a lot of work as a special. As well as *Little Dorrit* and *The Fool*, he has shot stills on most of Richard Goodwin's co-productions with John Brabourne, including *Murder on the Orient Express* (1974) and *Death on the Nile* (1978), as well as on David Lean's *A Passage to India* (1984).

Photograph 16
Sarah Pickering in *Little Dorrit*: this picture was used for the film's poster, on the book jacket of the Penguin special film edition of the Charles Dickens novel, and on the LP cover of the original soundtrack recording. *Little Dorrit* is a film in two parts, each three hours long. The film was made at Sands Films Studios, Rotherhithe, London. It took two years to prepare, 135 days to shoot and was nine months in post-production. There are 250 actors in the cast. It was shot entirely in the studio.

Some famous specials

I find it often surprises, even annoys, my students (and other photographers too) when they discover just how many well-known and respected photographers have spent time working in the movies. 'Stills work is just a form of licensed plagiarism,' they say. 'How can you be serious about it?'

In recent years it has, sadly, become standard practice in colleges where photography is taught to evaluate a photographer's contribution to the medium solely in terms of his so-called 'personal' work and to denigrate his work done on assignment. It is a fashion which has produced some incredible distortions of fact.

Many famous photo-essays which were originally shot on assignment have now been redefined as 'personal' work. People don't like to be told, for instance, that a good number of Robert Frank's pictures from his remarkable book *The Americans* were first published in *Esquire* magazine, or that Cartier-Bresson enjoyed a long and fruitful relationship with *Holiday* magazine and that he shot many pictures in colour.

To trumpet 'personal' work at the expense of 'commercial' work is, I think, dangerous. I hear them doing it in lecture theatres, I hear it on the lips of students, I read it in the comments of critics, I even hear photographers using it as an excuse for turning in bad work. Surely the significant distinction between commercial work and self-originated work is simply one of function?

In my view, a photographer who withholds that part of himself which is 'personal' from the work he does for others is not being honest, either with himself or with those who pay him. So when people ask me if the work I do on assignment in the movies is 'serious' work, I say: 'Of course.'

A man from whom I have learned a lot, one of photography's great teachers, is David Hurn, the Magnum photographer who started the school of Documentary Photography at Newport. I remember it amused him greatly when I told him that the first time I saw his byline was not alongside one of his famous 60s pictures of the MG car-owners' club dinner or the Soho strippers but alongside a picture of Sean Connery on the cover of the paperback edition of Ian Fleming's *From Russia with Love* (1963). It was in 1964, I was twelve years old, and I remember the book well because it had been punctured with holes to make it look like movie footage. Another of the pictures on that jacket showed two scantily clad women wrestling

Photograph 17
A little of Venice in Borehamwood. Seconds later the studio was filled with smoke to simulate swirling fog and hide the poor props man who was providing propulsion.

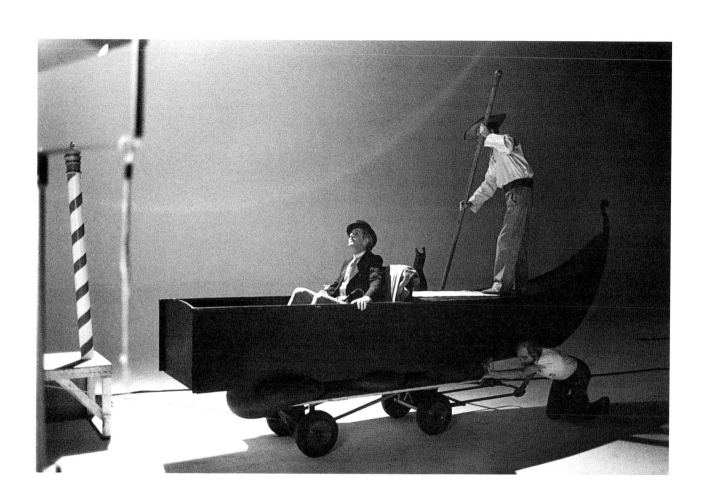

and, because of this, my headmaster had banned the book and I was forced to read it clandestinely under the blankets by torchlight.

Hurn didn't just work on the Bond films; he worked on *El Cid* with Charlton Heston (1961), *Waterloo* with Rod Steiger (1970) and on several features for Ken Russell including *French Dressing* (1963), *The Devils* (1970) and *The Boyfriend* (1971). He also did more than 125 colour front covers worldwide of Jane Fonda in *Barbarella* (1967), and that must be some kind of record.

Many famous photographers have worked in the movies and it's sad that you do not see much of their film work in their monographs. I can only assume that when sorting through their lifetime's work, choosing images for posterity, most photographers prefer to select from pictures done on self-originated projects rather than invite criticism for being incapable of originality.

It's sad because much good work has been done by stillsmen. Among the names you might expect to find on a list of those who have stood around on film sets are:

Dennis Stock, who photographed Humphrey Bogart as Captain Queeg in *The Caine Mutiny* (1954) and whose pictures of James Dean, taken in 1955 at the time of *Rebel Without a Cause*, are now widely used on posters and in advertisements.

The two Sterns: Phil, who served as a 'special' or unit stillsman on more than 200 feature films, including *Guys and Dolls* (1955) and *In Cold Blood* (1967),[5] and Bert (no relation) whose 'last sitting' pictures of Marilyn Monroe taken in 1962 have been reproduced many times. Bert Stern also photographed Elizabeth Taylor and Richard Burton in *Cleopatra* (1963).

Eve Arnold, too, has a memorable collection of Monroe pictures and she photographed Burton, on *Becket* (1964). Robert Doisneau shot stills for Bertrand Tavernier on *Sunday in the Country* (1984), and Mary Ellen Mark photographed Cher and Meryl Streep in *Silkwood* (1983).

And then there was Weegee, of course.

But there are some names you might *not* expect to see on that list: Edward Sherriff Curtis, best known for his documentation of North American Indians between 1896 and 1919 (contained in an archive of some 40,000 negatives), photographed *The Ten Commandments* (1923) for Cecil B. DeMille, and did portraits of Johnny Weismuller in *Tarzan The Ape Man* (1932) and of Gary Cooper in *The Plainsman* (1936).

Edward Steichen, who organised that great photographic exhibition 'The

Family of Man' (1955), visited Hollywood throughout the 1930s on assignment for Condé Nast and produced some memorable portraits of Douglas Fairbanks, Gloria Swanson and Marlene Dietrich.

W. Eugene Smith, famous for his classic photo-essays in *Life* magazine and for his campaigning book *Minamata* about the effects of pollution from a Japanese fertiliser factory on the health of a fishing community, photographed Gregory Peck in *Twelve O'Clock High* (1950) and Charlie Chaplin in *Limelight* (1952).

Larry Burrows, also of *Life* magazine and who was killed covering the Vietnam war, did stills of Laurence Olivier in *Richard III* (1956).

Don McCullin, another photographer of wars, shot stills for John Irvin's *Hamburger Hill* (1987).

Czech photographer Josef Koudelka, who has for long been the guru of many purists, worked alongside Eve Arnold as a 'special' on the Baryshnikov movie *White Nights* (1985).

And Cartier-Bresson himself turned out to shoot pictures of Marilyn Monroe on *The Misfits* (1961). His portrait of her remains in print in that excellent Thames and Hudson book which contains over 200 of his portraits.

Cartier-Bresson, as every photography student knows, defined 'the decisive moment'.[6] He it was who wrote that 'Photography is the simultaneous recognition, in a fraction of a second, of the significance of an event as well as of a precise organisation of forms which give that event its proper expression.' But what people sometimes forget is that in the same essay (in fact in the second paragraph) he acknowledges that he learned 'to look, and to see' in the movies.

So let's hear no more about stills being work for second-rate snappers. Stillsmen are photographers too!

A five picture theory

Someone else who worked as a stillsman, though for a short time only, was the Hungarian 'father of photo-journalism', Stefan Lorant,[7] the editor of such pioneering weekly magazines as *Münchner Illustrierte* in Germany before World War II, and *Picture Post* in the UK during it. He worked in the film industry as a young man, first in Vienna and then in Berlin. He quickly became a cameraman and then a director, and made seven films before giving it all up and going into publishing.

I mention this because it was through analysing Lorant's and other (later) editors' layouts in picture magazines that David Hurn developed the theory of storytelling in pictures which he taught at Newport.[8] Interestingly, in the context of this book, Hurn's Five Picture Theory also has much in common with the language of film-making, as we shall see.

Hurn's Five Picture Theory goes like this:

Most picture stories contain some or all of five kinds of picture. If you can learn to shoot each one and master it you will have at your fingertips the tools of a picture language similar to basic grammar or musical notation. The first three kinds are 'observed' pictures where the photographer aims to make order in the frame out of the chaos of the world and at least give the illusion that any human subjects in his pictures are not aware of being photographed. These are:

1. *A person working*, somebody doing something.
2. *A relationship*. This might be two or more people doing something together – arguing or laughing perhaps – or two shapes which play off one against the other, or even people/objects between whom no relationship actually exists except for the one imposed on them by the way the photographer has seen them.
3. *An establishing picture* or GV (general view), establishing both mood and location.

   Then come the pictures which are not 'observed' so much as 'directed':
4. *A set-up picture*, a formal portrait or a studio shot. Here the photographer is in control of every detail of the subject's appearance.
5. *A close-up*, often of some small detail which will look surprising when seen enlarged beyond life-size when printed.

Photograph 18
Man at work: at Elstree an executive producer checks out the script. The rest he is leaning against, provided by the wardrobe department, is for the use of artistes who are dressed in costumes of such elaborate splendour that they must not risk damaging them by sitting down.

Playing tunes

Having mastered these five pictures the photographer can – like a musician playing a tune – then apply them to telling his story. A story is defined as a grouping of pictures which complement each other in a way which generates an effect greater than the sum of its parts. Before shooting any pictures the photographer must analyse his subject, deciding upon its visual strengths and weaknesses. Something to avoid is the 'point' picture, a picture that merely explains what could be written just as well in a caption.

When shooting a picture story you have to be aware of something we call 'pace' because if you shoot all your pictures from the same distance with the same lens the pictures will kill each other when set down together on the layout. To pace a story well you need wide pictures, middle-distance pictures and close-up pictures. You need vertical pictures and horizontal pictures, you need graphic pictures and quiet pictures, busy pictures and clean pictures, action pictures and so on.

Film-making is similar. Okay, the pictures move and there is a soundtrack, but many of the same rules apply and, if anything, the conventional approach to telling stories with film is even more rigid than the one I have described for storytelling with stills, if only because it is so much more expensive if you get it wrong.

In film the director begins with a master shot, actors come and go, the atmosphere and mood are established. (When shooting stills on a film set, the period when the master shot is being set – which usually takes a very long time – often provides an opportunity for the stillsman to make himself known to the actors.) Then the camera moves in on the action to see who is saying what and to whom (relationship shot). This is a busy time for the stillsman since it is now that he must shoot his two-shots and close-ups, both during rehearsal and during the performance. (Two-shots and close-up head shots being the two kinds of picture which are most in demand by newspapers and magazines.) There will be plenty of close-ups, cutaways and reaction shots to follow before the scene is complete and, if the crew manages to get three minutes of footage (at its cut length) into the can, then they will reckon to have had a good day. Oh yes, making films is a slow and painstaking business. It is not a job for the impatient.

Photograph 19
Establishing shot: St George's Hall, Liverpool, doing service in *Testimony* for the 1948 Moscow conference at which Zhdanov denounced Shostakovich and tore up his Ninth Symphony.

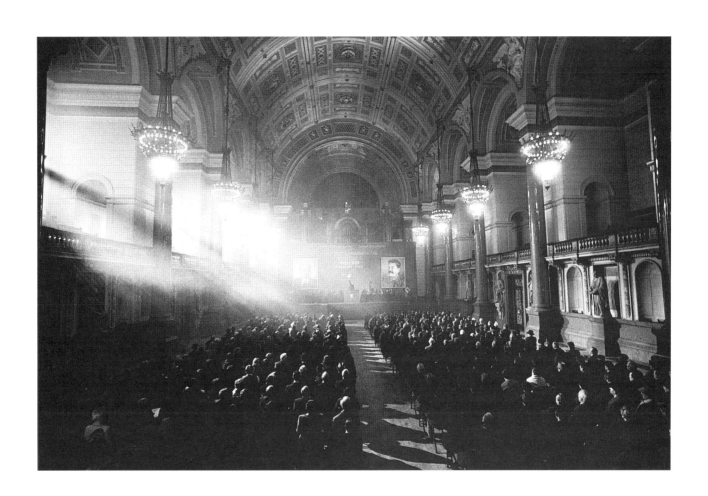

Welcome the stillsman!

The stills photographer is the only member of a film crew whose work is *not* essential to the job in hand – that of getting footage in the can – so, unless he is careful, he can easily find he becomes the scapegoat for all the many tensions which spill over while the other members of a crew go about their work. It's so easy to be in the way!

Boom swingers tread on your toes; focus pullers give you the elbow; sparks humping blondes shove you from behind (it's not as bad as it sounds – see p. 99); and actors who fluff their lines bark: 'How on *earth* do you expect me to work while I am being photographed?'

Come the publicity meeting, though, three months before the film goes on release and long after the filming (or 'principal photography' as it is called) is over, then the stillsman is suddenly the *most* important man on the production … until, that is, he is asked: 'Where's the picture of so-and-so?' Somehow, it's never good enough to say: 'Don't you remember, I was sent off the set that day?'

That stills are essential to the successful promotion of a film is never questioned. That a stills photographer should be tolerated on a film set often is. Publicity people want still pictures in black and white and in colour of every set-up filmed… they can't have enough. Getting them, though, that's the problem.

Earlier I described the way stills *should* be done – how, at the end of each set-up, the movie camera is rolled back and the actors asked to 'do it one more time for stills'. Well, in my experience this rarely happens. First assistants, whose job it is to give the order for proceedings to be held up while the stillsman gets his picture, have lost the habit. Maybe I've been unlucky, maybe in Britain the industry is so insecure and so underfunded that all anyone can think about is getting on with shooting footage in case someone stops the flow of money before the film is finished.

Anyway, take it from me, if you want to shoot stills these days you have got to learn to do it *around* everyone else and *in spite of* everyone else, and only intervene to beg a set-up when all else has failed. This requires considerable skill and, for me anyway, it is in the exercise of this skill that the job-satisfaction is to be had.

Doing the deal

It's time to come clean. So far, I have described myself as a unit stillsman, a title which squares with my screen credit, but there are a lot of old-time movie technicians who would take exception to me using this title because it is not my practice to work every day on a film set during the period of principal photography. Yes, I shoot the unit stills but I am not, in the traditional sense of the term, a unit stillsman.

I came into the film industry at a time when producers, ever trimming their budgets, began to turn their attention to the cost of producing stills. They realised that, if they hired their stillsman only for the days of a shoot that were most likely to produce the pictures which would actually get published, then considerable savings might be made. So, in an industry which for years had been closed to outsiders, there were now at last some openings for photographers like me.

The way I work is this:

Some weeks before principal photography commences, I am sent a script, a schedule and a provisional cast list. These I scrutinise carefully. Then, at a meeting with the director, the producer and the unit publicist, I discuss the specific days when I should attend the set. Obviously it is important to shoot pictures of big-name actors, but it is also important to understand what the film is *about* and to select some days which might produce the kind of stills which establish the mood or flavour of the film.

Sometimes I am told the limit of the stills budget so that I can charge my fee as a day-rate (many producers will want to retain copyright of the stills and I have to take this into account when calculating fees), but the rate I charge isn't necessarily the sole determining factor over whether or not I get the job; connections are important too, particularly with the picture editors of newspapers and magazines. In due course a stills schedule is arrived at and, if approved, I am up and running.

The first day on the set is always a tense occasion because the way a stillsman works then sets his working pattern for the days to come. As time goes on these first days get easier because there is an increasing number of old faces to greet, but at the beginning of a shoot everyone is trying to make his mark and create the right impression.

How is it done?

The accepted practice for shooting stills is that the stillsman puts his camera into something called a 'blimp'. A blimp is a soundproof box, and the idea is that he can click away during a take (when the camera is rolling and the sound recordist 'turning over') without any risk that the noise of his camera will distract the actors or be heard on the soundtrack.

Well! The first time I saw a blimp, the first thing that came into my head was the old joke about the fellow who tried picking his nose with his gloves on. I just couldn't believe that anyone expected me to perform with my camera locked up inside that thing. Monstrous things they are, blimps, and any gain achieved by using one is, in my experience, far outweighed by its almost total lack of manoeuvrability. It has been a great relief to me that, mostly, I have been able to get by without one.

The truth is that of the five pictures outlined in the Five Picture Theory (p. 54), the stillsman shoots only three: the head shot (close-up), the two-shot (relationship) and the wide shot (establishing). Now, when shooting a close-up head shot the photographer is so close to a performer that were he to attempt to shoot during a take he would be compelled to move into the actor's eyeline which, in the scale of sins likely to get you sent off the set, is at least as bad as firing the shutter during a take. So, blimp or no blimp, you have to shoot head shots during rehearsal.

The same rule applies for shooting the two-shot, which is twice as difficult as the head shot because now there are two sets of actor's eyelines to be aware of.

Which leaves the wide shot. Here the blimp *can* be useful, particularly when you are out on location and you need to capture action. With the principal artistes all wired with radio mikes and a long way from the camera, you'd have thought that out of doors the sound of a camera shutter would go unnoticed; but believe me, it doesn't. You can be sure there's always a boom swinger somewhere nearby recording atmospheric sound. So before abandoning the blimp, the stillsman must always check with the sound mixer that it is safe to do so.

If a stillsman is sent off the set for firing during a take, it may be a very long time before he is allowed back again.

Photograph 20
On *Testimony* I was roped in as an extra to operate a movie camera in a Russian film studio. I kept my Olympus under my costume and stole the odd still or two, including this one.

So when can the stillsman take pictures?

The truth is that it is only on rare occasions that the stillsman *needs* to fire his shutter during the take. Standing as near to the movie camera as possible, even squatting on the front of the camera dolly, the stillsman shoots most of his pictures during the few seconds – and they are *very* few – at the start of a shot when all the actors are on their marks waiting for the director to shout 'Action', or in the brief moment at the end of the shot, after the director has shouted 'Cut' and before the actors relax. If, at the end of the shot, the stillsman is lucky enough to catch the artiste's eye, the artiste might just hold his or her expression and gesture long enough for him to fire off a couple of frames (Ben Kingsley, for instance, is a gem at this), but mostly performers don't catch the stillsman's eye and if he wants another chance to get his stills he has to pray that somewhere there's been a cock-up and the director will decide to 'go again'.

Come to think of it, the stillsman is probably the only crew member who spends most of his time praying for other people to cock-up!

Remember, for each set-up the stillsman is aiming for pictures in both colour and black and white and there is rarely a chance to get off more than two or three frames. I usually shoot colour first since, in a fix, it is always possible to make a black and white picture from the colour transparency (but not of course the other way round). I use two cameras, one containing black and white film, the other colour, and (very slowly so as not to cause a distraction) I swap them over during the take. Generally it's 'not done' to try for a few extra frames by using a motorwind in these situations, since most people are tense and trying to concentrate and the noise is considered distracting.

Other opportunities for shooting stills do occur during rehearsals and line-ups, but it's rare for the lighting to be correct at these times and, if they are not replaced by stand-ins, the artistes are often carrying scripts, wearing spectacles, drinking tea or having their make-up attended to. And if the artistes *are* all right, then you can bet your life there's an electrician in the background adjusting a lamp or a props man circulating with a bee gun.

Believe me, the opportunities for shooting stills which look like the footage are few and far between.

Photograph 21
Ben Kingsley as Dmitri
Shostakovich in *Testimony*

And if that isn't enough …

Talk about trying to do your job with one hand tied behind your back! You haven't heard the half of it yet …

In photography there is something called an 'f stop', a hole in the lens the size of which can be adjusted to control the amount of light entering the camera. Wide open the stop is f2 (or thereabouts), fully closed the stop is f16. The f stop doesn't just alter the amount of light which reaches the film, it also controls 'depth of field', which is the area either side of the point of focus – the actor's eyeball in a close-up – which is also in focus. At f16 the actor's ears and the tip of his nose might be sharp, but at f2 even his eyebrows are likely to be unsharp.

Obviously photographers like the chance to work at the smaller f stops so as to benefit from the maximum depth of field. However, recent technical developments in the manufacture of film emulsions have led to the production of some very high-speed movie stock. ('Speed' is the term used to describe a film emulsion's sensitivity to light. The faster the film, the less light is needed to expose it correctly.) These high-speed emulsions are now very popular with film-makers because they save money on the lighting and electricity budgets; but the use of them makes a stillsman's life a misery. *His* film (Tungsten Ektachrome) has a speed of 160asa, while the latest movie stock is rated at 500asa, one and a half stops more tolerant of low light.

Light levels on film sets are often so low that stillsmen are obliged to shoot their pictures with the camera set on 1/15 second at f2. Normally you would not attempt to photograph even a slow-moving subject using a shutter speed longer than 1/125 second, and most photographers reckon they can't hold the camera steady for shutter speeds longer than 1/60 second, but to find yourself working on 1/15 second!

I attempt to overcome this problem by fixing the camera to a monopod, a tripod being out of the question because it is too bulky. As it happens, my particular monopod has become something of a trademark. Being 6ft 6in tall, and fully retractable monopods not extending beyond 6ft, I am obliged to use a two-piece pod, a great pole of a thing which makes me look like some kind of hi-tech shepherd. You can imagine the ribaldry it generates among the crew!

There's no pleasing them

I am having lunch with the picture editor of a quality broadsheet. We talk for a while about a feature he is running on 'forgotten' Hollywood stillsman Phil Stern. Then he says: 'Why are *today's* movie stills always so bad? I can never find anything really good for our screen pages.' He says all he ever gets from film publicity people are grainy transparencies duped to a fuzz or flat prints made from copy-negs. 'Don't they *care* about their movies, these film people? How can they expect *us* to care when it's obvious from the quality of what they send us that they don't care themselves?'

He's right, of course. The movie still is a low-status picture and, these days, rarely credited to its photographer. And one thing is certain: it will remain a humble thing just so long as nothing is done to persuade *all* movie people of its importance. It's not just the publicists who are to blame: they have their troubles, too many cooks for one thing. All those actors who affect to hate being photographed and discourage stills by rehearsing with overcoats over their costumes or with silly hats on; producers who trim their stills budgets to such a degree that significant scenes are often allowed to pass by unrecorded; stars with stills vetoes written into their contracts; assistant directors who fail to appreciate that if they give the stillsman even thirty seconds (rather than two seconds) to shoot an important picture he can produce thirty original transparencies to satisfy thirty different picture editors instead of just one transparency which, if it isn't scratched in the lab (and it probably will be), will then have to be duped. Oh yes, the publicity people have their troubles all right.

The phone rings. It's the picture editor of a popular tabloid. He is, he says, looking at my stills from Tony Palmer's *Testimony*. 'I wanted you to know that these are some of the finest movie stills I have ever seen,' he says. 'Really!' he adds, as if I won't believe him.

'Well, thank you,' I say, distinctly chuffed.

'But I'm afraid we've butchered them. I hope you won't hold it against me. They're simply too good for us. One day perhaps I'll work for a publication that cares about pictures and I'll be able to lay you out a really nice spread. Anyway I thought I'd just ring …'

Decent of him.

Approximately f2 portraits

The actor knight and the bee gun

Probably the most difficult job I had on Christine Edzard's *The Fool* was photographing Michael Hordern, though it was no fault of his. The schedule had been changed because bad weather had lost Edzard one of her few location days and I was left with just one day in which to get a much needed still of the actor knight in character.

The set, one of Sands Films' smaller studios, was beautiful: the green room (actor's rest room) of a Victorian theatre. It was long and narrow with windows at intervals all down one side. The lighting cameraman, Robin Vidgeon, had lit it exquisitely. Outside the windows a battery of 5ks (large quartzlights), slightly blued to look like daylight, sent beams of simulated sunlight slanting into the gloomy interior. What Vidgeon had done was to create a strongly atmospheric light for people to move in. At any given moment no single actor would (in photographic terms) be perfectly lit but as they moved about, in and out of the sunlight – now over-exposed (bright), now under-exposed (dark) – an image would gradually be assembled in the audience's mind and establish the desired mood. To avoid excess contrast in the sunlit parts and to diffuse the light so that some of it spilt into the shaded parts, Vidgeon squirted the room with the wafted smoke of incense burnt in a bee gun.

It was a skilled piece of work, and subtle – but it was absolutely appalling for stills!

In the dark parts of the room it was simply too dark to take pictures and in the bright parts, where there was just enough light, it was too contrasty (still transparency emulsions being less tolerant of lighting contrast than movie negative emulsions). All I could do was attempt to photograph the artistes during the fleeting moments when they were *halfway* into the sunlight, but this wasn't going to be easy unless they stood still long enough not to blur.

And sure enough, as if to confirm my worst fears, when I watched the rehearsal I saw that Michael Hordern, who played the part of the irate theatre manager Mr Tatham, was required to walk up and down constantly, waving his arms about and ranting.

People often ask why stillsmen need to take so many pictures. The answer is that, when required to work in conditions like these, for every roll exposed only a handful of frames will be usable.

Photograph 22
Michael Hordern as
Mr Tatham in *The Fool*

Photograph 23 Max Wall as Flintwinch in *Little Dorrit*

Photograph 24 Derek Jacobi as Mr Frederick in *The Fool*

Photograph 25 Rosalie Crutchley: the Magnate from the Bench's wife in *Little Dorrit*

Photograph 26 Alec Guinness as William Dorrit in *Little Dorrit*

Photograph 27 Don Henderson as the blind stagehand in *The Fool*

Photograph 28 Miranda Richardson as Columbine in *The Fool*

Catch a gawping star

If I have a mission as a stillsman it is to persuade actors, producers and film publicists everywhere (especially film publicists) that the best publicity still is the picture which communicates something about the *meaning* of the film. This is not an easy picture to take because it's not always a picture that can be planned, set up or scheduled, but that doesn't mean that you shouldn't try. If your ambitions for good promotional photographs begin and end with a lit colour portrait of the star gawping into the lens, then the best promotional pictures will always remain unshot.

The most important question anyone publicising a film drama must ask is not 'Who is *in* this film?' but 'What is this film *about*?' The action is always more interesting than the actors, and a single picture which sums up the feel of a drama is in my view worth a whole shooting gallery of actors' mug shots.

Because the picture of Little Dorrit walking in the Marshalsea yard (p. 49) is exactly this kind of mood picture, I am for ever grateful to Christine Edzard for encouraging her distributors to use it on the film's poster and handbill. 'What? A vertical picture on a poster? Unthinkable!' With all those stars at her disposal it was a brave decision.

And the same goes for Ken Russell, who encouraged me to publicise *The Mystery of Doctor Martinu* with that picture of all those extras running on the beach with their black umbrellas (p. 45). Once the film was edited that scene lasted no more than two or three seconds; but when the still of it was run across eight columns in the *Guardian*, people wrote to me asking for prints. And it was brave of the publicity people too, especially when you consider what a temptation all those pictures of Hannah King in the nude must have presented. But sense prevailed. Everyone realised the truth of the thing: that to promote a film about a composer's dreams with a picture of a naked lady suggests that the scope of Martinu's imagination was limited to sexual fantasy.

Stills are a movie's shop window and the stillsman owes it to the cinemagoer to come up with something that gives a true impression of what the film is about. The story is just as important as who is acting in it, who they've been sleeping with lately or how rich they are. (Tell that to the editor of *Hello!*)

A musical interlude

Tony Palmer

Although he has made films on a variety of subjects, Tony Palmer is known principally for his TV documentaries and feature films about composers. As a man he has enough charm to start a migration and the most amazing recall for information. As a film-maker, these qualities translate into an exceptional gift for getting people to talk about themselves and a formidable talent for reassembling what they say into a sensible narrative.

Critics find his work difficult because it rarely conforms to the accepted norms of the 'biopic'. When telling a life story Palmer always weaves together the musical and the biographical elements to show how the one informs the other. He would not, I think, have much time for the view expressed by American photographer Garry Winogrand that 'The artist is irrelevant once the work exists.'[9]

In *Testimony*, for instance, he paints a picture of Shostakovich as a man of unconquerable spirit who survived despite the tyrannical demands of the dictator Stalin. In the two documentaries which won him the *Prix Italia* (Palmer is still the only director to have won it twice in succession), his view of Benjamin Britten[10] centres on the composer's love for Peter Pears, while William Walton[11] is seen as a man of humble origins who, despite incredible achievements, thought worthless most of what he had done.

Palmer thrives on controversy. His £7.25m nine-hour film of *Wagner*, which was 'dogged by financial crises and acrimonious discord'[12] and dubbed 'the most troubled film in the history of the British Film Industry,'[13] has yet to have a general cinema release in Britain even in its five-hour version, yet it won prizes for Best Drama at both the New York and London film festivals.

Palmer is the true successor to Ken Russell. Indeed, as a trainee he went to work at the BBC in order to be with Russell, an experience he describes as 'a wonderful nine months with Ken. It was absolutely hateful. I was brought to the depths of total desperation. I have never wanted to kill someone so many times in my life.'[14]

There have, I admit, been plenty of occasions when I might have said exactly the same about working for Palmer – but then perhaps you always feel that way about the people who inspire you the most.

Julian Bream

Before I got to work on any of Palmer's films, he asked me to fly with him to Italy and shoot some pictures for a book he was planning about the virtuoso concert guitarist Julian Bream.[15]

Bream is an unlikely character, an affable, roly-poly Londoner with a distaste for 'entourage', a fiercely independent spirit and a quite incredible ability to transport his audience during a performance. Despite his impeccable good manners he was at first, I think, a little suspicious of me. He doesn't like undue attention, and he was worried that I would dash about all the time firing flashbulbs. When he saw how quickly I could work and that I use flash only rarely, he soon relaxed and we became good friends – which was just as well since when hotels cocked up the booking arrangements we were sometimes obliged to share a room.

The five days we spent travelling through Italy in Bream's Volvo established a working pattern that continued on and off for the best part of a year. We attended recitals – on that trip Milan, Rome, Padua and Turin – always in front of packed and highly appreciative audiences, and visited the various composers from whom Bream was commissioning new works. In Rome we called on the German composer Hans Werner Henze who had just completed a guitar sonata entitled 'Royal Winter Music'. Palmer interviewed Bream as we drove, recording the conversation on tape for later transcription. We compiled a dummy (10,000 words and twenty photographs) and Palmer's literary agent quickly secured us a sizeable advance for the book.

During 1981 I travelled with Bream on solo tours to Rumania and Yugoslavia, to festivals in Edinburgh, Aldeburgh and Dartington, and on an ensemble tour with the Julian Bream Consort (along with tenor Robert Tear) to the Low Countries. I also went twice to the USA, first to New York and then California, and I learned Bream-speak: cigarettes are 'tubes of joy', fingers 'a bunch of bananas', spaghetti 'spag bol', mediaeval music 'the olde musicke racket', the Volvo 'a Swedish tank' and his guitar 'the box'. I even got into the habit of thanking waiters with a cheery 'gratsiozo'! I met and photographed a lot of musicians, including Peter Maxwell Davies, Michael Tippett and William Walton.

Photograph 30
Julian Bream in his dressing room at the Maltings, Snape

Holding a candle for spontaneity

One of the difficulties I face as a photographer of famous faces is in explaining the natural resistance I have to shooting set-up pictures.

It has always seemed to me that if a photograph is made in a fraction of a second then the fraction of a second recorded in the picture should be a significant fraction of a second. It matters very much to me that a picture is taken now and not ('Wait a beat,' as a director might say) … now! I abhor the photo-opportunity and the portrait session because I'm blowed if I am going to shoot pictures which look like the subject is admiring himself or herself in my mirror. I don't see myself as part of anybody's publicity machine. I want to shoot pictures which are spontaneous, which make the people in them look like they might to you, the viewer, if you just happened by at the time. I hate pictures which interrupt the action. That's not to say it isn't *possible* to produce lively, 'observed' pictures of people looking into the camera – some photographers do, though not many do it terribly well – but that is simply not the kind of picture that *I* want to make. I will try anything to avoid shooting set-ups.

The picture I did of Julian Bream with Sir William Walton (opposite) is a good example of this. The set-up prepared for us was two armchairs in a smart hotel room in Kensington. As the introductions were made, I could see we were edging towards a dead picture and I began to shoot straight away. But I was able to get off only one frame before Walton took his seat. This is it. I prefer it to all the formal pictures I was obliged to shoot, because of the twinkle in the old man's eye. There are those who would criticise it for the way the crockery on the table is distracting, or for the fact that the two men are too far apart or because the middle of the picture is empty. But I don't care, I think it's got spark.

On the other hand I would never try to read anything into the picture. You might, for instance, say that Walton is looking disapproving because Bream is drinking; or you might note that the picture was taken just a few months before Walton died and claim that, because he is looking over his shoulder like a man reviewing his life, the picture is in some way prophetic. Such analysis would be ridiculous.

It's just a lively, close picture of two famous men and I think it has life and I think it has intimacy.

Photograph 31
William Walton and
Julian Bream

New York

Palmer and I made a whistle-stop tour to New York to witness Bream's performance at the Avery Fisher Hall. I'm ashamed to say I had to lie to get a picture of the maestro at the concert, signing a piece of paper for the theatre management to say that I wouldn't take a flashgun into the hall. This picture (opposite) is the result of that deceit and is one of my favourite pictures from the book. It was made during the applause following encores when amateur flashes were popping all over the auditorium and my flash – fired in conjunction with a long exposure to get the blur of Bream's formal bow – was just one among many.

It was my first visit to New York and although Palmer insisted we had a walking race as, next morning, we made our way down Sixth Avenue, so that I was forced to appreciate it all at the double, I found I was dazzled by the place. It was November but the sky was a clear blue, the air crystal and every vista razor-sharp, a freak spell of summer polishing the crinkle of fallen leaves. Being among those buildings wasn't like being *next* to pieces of sculpture, it was like being *inside* one huge sculpture. I had never appreciated quite how big those skyblocks are, or how the light bouncing off them is fractured into geometric patterns creating a light show for pedestrians to walk in.

But we did not have long to play games and stare. In thirty hours we took in meetings with Bream's New York agent, the editor of *Guitar Review*, some officials at RCA records, an American accountant, and a Jewish manufacturer of guitar strings called Rose Augustine, who had perfected the art of burnishing the wire-wrapped bass strings so as to reduce the amount of squeak they can make.

As well as going to the concert we went to the post-concert party and we even found time, on our way back to the airport, to call in on Madame Stravinsky to sort out some details of the film Palmer was making about her late husband.[16] We returned to London on the same 747 we had come on, Palmer with an upset stomach from consuming too much cake and fresh orange juice, and me with Stravinsky's death mask in a box on my lap. On the aeroplane Palmer showed me an essay entitled 'Wagner, The Photographic Purposes of the Film', written by the cameraman he had just signed up for his nine-hour epic – Vittorio Storaro.

Photograph 32
Julian Bream at the Avery Fisher Hall, New York

Vittorio Storaro

I am not at liberty to describe what was in that essay (Palmer swore me to secrecy); anyway, I haven't a copy so it's probably just as well that I don't try to quote it from memory. What I can do is describe a little of the way this triple Oscar-winning[17] lighting cameraman went about his business.

A London gaffer (chief electrician) once explained to me what lighting is all about: 'You've got three lights,' he said, 'that's all there is. There's key light, there's back light and there's fill-in. Key light imitates the sun, back light puts a rim round things and fill-in takes the contrast out of the key light.'

He was right, of course, but to watch Storaro work you'd never guess it. For a start Storaro is not frightened to use very low light levels and he mixes a concoction of flat, soft light with a very small amount of bright, strongly directional light. His light always imitates natural sources like windows or candelabra, yet all the time he seems acutely aware of the particular mood he is trying to create.

For the directional light he uses carbon-rod burning arc lights and for the soft light 'Skypans' or 'Nine-lights' (large dishes containing many light bulbs). Like a waiter at high table serving awkward guests he filters unwanted light from the scene; his sets are hung with flags (wired lengths of black cloth of many and varying sizes), eight-by-four foot sheets of polystyrene, and – on tall flag stands – gauze, scrim and frosted paper. It is a light meant for people to move in and he is very precise about how much of it he needs and where it should go.

So precise that more than once I saw him whip open his long black coat during a take and – out of the frame – move along beside an artiste using his brilliant white roll-neck sweater to reflect just a little more light into the face. He is, at least in part, a showman. He is very much the father figure of his all-Italian crew and, although a perfectionist, his nature is generous.

Once, while filming beside the Grand Canal in Venice, a disruptive vagrant wandered onto the set. Instead of getting angry, Storaro walked over to the man and engaged him in conversation. Then, ever so gently, he edged the man into a café, bought him a drink and sat with him until he had calmed down.

Photograph 33
Vittorio Storaro on the set of *Wagner*, Vienna 1982

Photograph 34 Yehudi Menuhin

Photograph 35 Mitsuko Uchida

Virtuosi

On two occasions Palmer summoned me to a church off the Portobello Road in West London to shoot stills of concert performers he was filming for TV profiles.

On the first occasion it was Mitsuko Uchida,[18] the Japanese pianist, playing Mozart concertos with the English Chamber Orchestra. I sat at the end of her Steinway, between the violins and the violas, and shot my pictures during rehearsals. In particular I remember K467, well known to filmgoers as the theme music for Bo Widerberg's *Elvira Madigan* (1967). She is an expressive performer, wonderful to photograph, conducting from the piano and standing up from time to time to coax the orchestra by chopping the air with what I can only describe as a kind of karate. I wonder how much money Palmer might have made had he auctioned my seat that day?

No one could have afforded the ticket I had for the second visit I made to that church. Palmer's profile of Yehudi Menuhin, *A Family Life* (1990), is in my view the best of all his film biographies, even though Menuhin came out against it and managed to delay the publication of the accompanying book, *A Family Portrait* (Faber, 1991). This, I suppose, is the central dilemma for all biographers of the living: with the full blessing of your subject you tell your story using the words of his friends, family and colleagues, only to find that the views expressed are unacceptable to him. I have no idea whether or not Palmer's film of Menuhin is truthful; all I can say is that I find it sympathetic and, in the blessed absence of a publicist's rose-tinted filter, convincing.

Among several remarkable performances in the film, Menuhin gives a magical rendition of Elgar's violin concerto which, as it happens, is the piece he was playing when I photographed him. Considering that he has been playing it for sixty years, ever since he performed it under Elgar's own baton, I was greatly impressed that he didn't simply dash it off. He was determined to render it anew and kept urging the orchestra to 'try it this way, just try.'

A Family Life was lit by Nic Knowland, Palmer's principal cameraman. All I had to do was decide whether to show the maestro with his eyes shut (his normal playing attitude), or open.

I wonder: must photographs of the famous *always* confirm what we already know?

Testimony

Nic Knowland's way of working is about as different from Vittorio Storaro's as could be and yet the results he achieves are often just as breathtaking. Where Storaro sometimes achieves only five or six set-ups in a day, Knowland regularly turns in over twenty. Palmer likes to work quickly and Knowland delivers the goods. It was, for example, a truly remarkable feat by any standards that principal photography on *Testimony*, a two and a half hour wide-screen film, was completed in under five weeks.

Testimony is the story of Dmitri Shostakovich (Ben Kingsley). It is a visual treat. Shot in black and white, it has in it all of what one might recognise as Palmer's favourite imagery. The camera is never still; it spins and turns, dancing round the performers in long seamless takes. Many scenes are back-lit and there's oodles of smoke. Light cuts into the picture in great shafts, candles gutter, wax drips in dollops on bare table-tops. Trains belch clouds of steam, thundering footsteps echo round the auditorium and blood drips down the screen. You sit in your seat menaced by the music and the tormented lives you have come to share.

Nearly all of this was achieved, not in Leningrad or Moscow, but in Wigan. Yes, Wigan. Using a redundant mill and the bleak northern landscape, Palmer recreated Stalin's Russia.

Wigan Corporation lent a big old house, in which some of the least decayed rooms were hired out for local functions, to provide sets for many of the interior scenes. Indeed I recall one occasion when the banqueting room was so full of film smoke that it set off the fire alarm and there was a panic to get the crew out and the place aired before a party arrived to attend a wedding dinner on the very spot where only minutes before Stalin (Terence Rigby) had fallen dead out of his bed. St George's Hall, Liverpool, provided the venue for the 1948 Moscow conference at which Zhdanov (John Shrapnel) denounced Shostakovich and tore up his Ninth Symphony, and the Lakeside Railway on Windermere did service as the location for the trickiest night-time tracking shot I have ever seen attempted, which involved a Panaglide camera on a railway wagon, a steam locomotive, a fall of real snow, a large pleasure yacht, an exploding bust of Stalin, lady wrestler Mitzi Mueller as a pornographic nun and comedian Frank Carson telling one-liners.

Photograph 36 Colin Hurst in *Testimony*

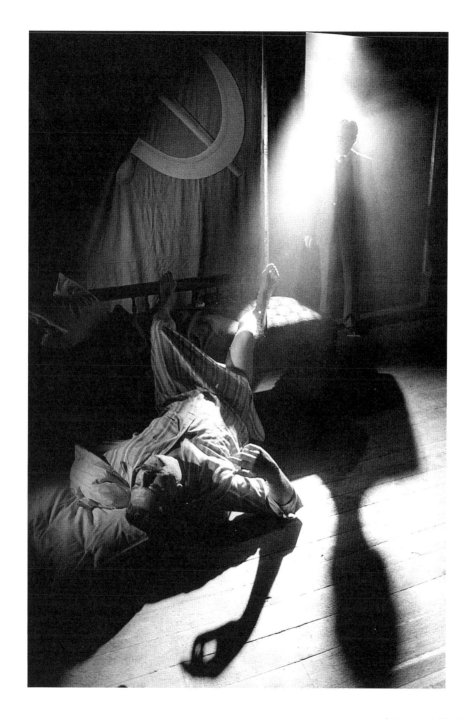

Photograph 37 *Testimony*: the death of Stalin

Crewspeak PG

James and Mary Jane

Ever since I saw him play opposite Rita Tushingham in the Tony Richardson film *A Taste of Honey* (1961), I have enormously enjoyed the work of actor Murray Melvin (opposite).

I have written a (never to be broadcast, it seems) radio play for Murray. As a work of literature it is difficult to categorise: let's just say that in the scheme of things it fits somewhere about halfway between, er … *Waiting for Godot* and *Hitchhiker's Guide to the Galaxy*. Huh! Melvin plays a Guardian Angel sent to earth to make sure that a predestined liaison between James, a mill engineer, and Mary Jane, the mill owner's delectable daughter, is properly consummated. The proceedings are recorded on film. The play opens with the Guardian Angel feeding sexy dreams to James as he sleeps in an armchair beside his engine while, in the background, a crew of cherubs chatters in esoteric film-speak.

1st CHERUB: (distant, Cockney) Do you want me to kiss his whatsisname with this, Guv?

2nd CHERUB: (nearer, posh Cockney) No, no. No inkie dinks today cherub. It's ten Ks I need. Finger-of-God lighting. We want a brute up a tower and lotsa smoke. Don't overdo it, we don't want a pea-souper. Good job he's a Catholic, eh Guv'nor?

GDN ANGEL: What?

2nd CHERUB: I said it's a good job this geezer's a Catholic. He'll be used to the pong of the smoke like, what wiv the incense an' all.

GDN ANGEL: (sharply) That's enough! Just get on.

2nd CHERUB: (chastened) Oooh! Don't get yer knickers in a twist. (Bossy, giving instructions to his crew) Let's have that mizar on a plate with a snoot. Put a single up that pup behind. Gimme a Charlie bar over here. No! Not the ulcer. That Blonde needs a yash and give a hand on the tower, will you! And a snatch block for the Best Boy. Put that pup on a turtle and … hurry it up, will you! I want the three legs on a rolling spider.

3rd CHERUB: How d'you want these barn doors? English or Chinese?

Photograph 38
Murray Melvin as a film editor in *Testimony*

Glossary

Perhaps the fact that the *Radio Times* would have to publish the following glossary before anyone could understand what is going on explains why the play has not yet been broadcast.

KISS: To shine a beam of light so that it just brushes an artiste's WHATSISNAME (this could be any part of the anatomy, exactly *which* part will most likely be obvious to the parties involved, otherwise a more specific term would be used).

INKIE DINK: A 300 watt tungsten lamp with a freznel lens.

TEN K: A large 10 kilowatt spot lamp, not to be confused with the larger 22 kilowatt carbon-rod burning DC arc lamp known as the BRUTE. Sometimes the sun is referred to as 'the big brute in the sky', especially when filming is held up because of cloud cover.

SMOKE: Smoke produced by burning incense in a bee-gun, a job for an expert. Recently a vegetable 'instant smoke' has been produced which comes in metal canisters; some cameramen favour it as it is easier to control the amount used. Smoke is used as a special effect (in this case to create beams of light) or to soften the contrast between a light area and a darker one.

MIZAR: A 500 watt tungsten lamp with a freznel lens.

PLATE: A weighted short lamp stand designed to hold a lamp a few inches above the floor.

SNOOT: Hollow tapering tube which fits over the lens of a lamp to create a disc of light.

SINGLE: A wire gauze which fits over the front of a lamp and cuts down the amount of light by one stop. A DOUBLE cuts the light by two stops.

PUP: A 1 kilowatt tungsten lamp with a freznel lens.

CHARLIE BAR: A kind of FLAG (sheet of black cloth on a wire frame), only it is made of a long thin piece of plywood painted black. It is placed in between a lamp and some part of the subject which the lamp is lighting, to offer a shadow. It is called a Charlie bar, I was told, because it 'keeps the light off her Charlies'.

ULCER: A sheet of black-painted plywood with random jagged holes cut in it. It is used in front of a lamp to give the effect of light filtering through leaves. Sometimes a SPARK (electrician) has to jiggle it about to suggest that the leaves are rustling in a breeze. Not to be confused with a RUPTURED ULCER, which is an ulcer with irregular edges.

BLONDE: A 2 kilowatt tungsten flood lamp, painted yellow. Not to be confused with a REDHEAD, which is an 800 watt flood lamp, painted red.

YASH: A wooden frame, the lower part of which has in it a piece of wood or gauze or neutral density gel which prevents some of the light emitted by a lamp from falling on the subject – as in yashmak, the garment worn by women in the East to conceal the lower part of the face.

TOWER: A scaffolding tower, often as high as twenty feet, erected by RIGGERS (construction workers), on which a BRUTE or big HMI (quartzlight) will be placed.

BEST BOY: Second electrician.

TURTLE: A short, three-legged lamp stand.

BARN DOORS: Hinged sheet-metal flaps on a square frame, painted black and mounted on the front of a lamp.

Film vocabulary is suffused with *double entendre*, as witnessed here in the description of the way the barn doors are to be set. The two at the side can be pushed together to create a *vertical* slit of light (ENGLISH), or the top and bottom barn doors can be gradually closed to create a *horizontal* slit of light (CHINESE). If the whole frame is twisted and doors adjusted to create a *diagonal* beam of light, the cameraman will call for GLADYS ON A BIKE or perhaps a DAME EDNA. Enough!

Sands Films

Rotherhithe

To strangers, film studios are forbidding places, but for the people who work in them they are often more homely than home itself. You see, every time something big is budgeted and paid for there is always a bit left over which is quickly colonised by those who know how to make good use of it in some undetected corner.

By far the most agreeable of these corners is a cramped little room under the Bullhead studio at Sands Films, just a stone's throw from the River Thames at Rotherhithe. The damp floor is covered with duckboards, but it is cosy and someone has decorated its walls with half a dozen china plates borrowed from the props room next door. It is on two levels. Up the steps, a tall man has to be careful not to bump his head on rusty beams.

Here the camera crew and the sparks do some serious entertaining. Here is a fridge. Here the best boy presides, spending the proceeds of a discreet whip-round so that the regulars and their guests can enjoy a glass of something stimulating and take their pick from a selection of eatables: crabsticks, nuts, smoked salmon even. Here the stand-by with the dubious slogan on his T-shirt plays host to the film financier, the movie actor and the newspaper columnist in the kind of atmosphere which landlords of expensive theme bars can ever only dream about. And here, for me, is one of the best things about working in films.

It would be a lonely life working as a stills photographer in movies were it not for the fact that there is such a strong sense of camaraderie among film crews. Because he belongs to no particular department, the stillsman can enjoy a privileged position, being invited to spend his spare time as much with the director and the producer as with the make-up department and the construction crew. I have experienced no other working situation where it is possible to enjoy quite such a varied range of convivial company.

No one in his right mind would describe film-making – with its strict chain of command, its movement orders and its military-style call sheets – as an egalitarian activity, but at Sands Films, where Richard Goodwin and Christine Edzard created *Little Dorrit*,[19] *The Fool* and *As You Like It*, all on the thinnest of thin shoestrings, it sometimes feels as though it could be.

Photograph 39
Richard Goodwin, producer of *Little Dorrit*, *The Fool* and *As You Like It*, teamed up with executive producer John Brabourne in 1970 to make a string of stylish and successful Agatha Christie films, including *Murder on the Orient Express* and *Death on the Nile*, as well as David Lean's *A Passage to India*. He is a very practical man (note the blackened fingernail) and owns a Thames barge in which he travelled from London to Vienna, an adventure he described in a book and a TV series.

Sands Films

Sands Films is being lent to David Puttnam's Enigma company to make a television film but, despite the presence of many famous actors, the man from the press agency has come to interview Christine Edzard. 'She's a genius,' he tells me, 'and I told her so. Did you see *Little Dorrit*? Wow!' He is very impressed.

Edzard's secret is that she strives all the time to do more for her audience than merely satisfy its desire for spectacle. The key to everything she does is the depth of research she is prepared to undertake in order to achieve the required result; for she believes that there is more to creating the 'feel' of a film, whatever its period, than can ever be achieved by merely dressing people up.

Her 'feel' is not hired or painted on, it is something which is cumulative, built up over months, years even. She is uncompromising. That the thing must be right in every detail is a philosophy she extends to all aspects of the film-making process – from the pattern on the wallpaper she hangs in a Victorian parlour to the words she puts into her actors' mouths. She has her own picture research library, her own carpentry shop, her own plaster, metalwork, model-making, painting and costume production workshops, and a permanent staff of twenty-five who believe in the work just as much as she does and care every bit as much about 'getting it right'. Craftsmen like plasterer Richard Ferose who, for *The Fool* (set in 1857), reinvented a forgotten process for making green *scagliola* (artificial marble) and out of it moulded twenty-four Corinthian columns, each twelve feet high, for the sumptuous great drawing-room scene. Craftswomen like Barbara Sonnex who, with the other seamstresses, sewed by hand (strictly no machine-sewing allowed, even for the undergarments) over 180 costumes, forty of them ball gowns. All Edzard's people happily double up on jobs. Olivier Stockman, for instance, credited as film editor on *Little Dorrit*, also did the continuity, made ninety-three stove-pipe hats and, what's more, invented the front projection system used for the wide street scenes.[20]

Now the press agency man has taken his place in the lunch queue of costumed extras, and he is so busy telling everyone how he has just met the wonderful Christine Edzard that he completely fails to notice that it is she who is ladling out his potatoes.

Photograph 40
Cyril Cusack as the Ballad Seller in *The Fool*

104

Cameramen

The director of photography on *Little Dorrit* was Bruno de Keyser. On *The Fool* and *As You Like It* it was Robin Vidgeon. It is their lighting you have to admire in the stills.

Edzard works with camera equipment which Richard Goodwin acquired when MGM's Borehamwood studios closed in 1970. The BNC side-finder camera is so old-fashioned, Vidgeon reckons it is the only one still operating anywhere in the world. But Edzard doesn't need to work with a modern lightweight camera, for her style is not defined by flashy camera movements; indeed, it is rare for her to move the camera very much at all – a slight pan, say, a gentle track of a few feet – but she never zooms or jibs. What concerns her is that her actors are given the best possible chance, that they are encouraged to enjoy the natural flow of the action.

A film much loved by Edzard is *Sunday in the Country*,[21] lit by de Keyser, which is why she chose him for *Little Dorrit*. De Keyser is French and a terrible tease. (He was always accusing me of being a thief, hanging around his sets with nothing better to do than steal his Rembrandts.) Vidgeon, who has seen *Sunday in the Country* three times, says he admires the way the lighting looks so natural, 'almost as though there was nothing artificial about it at all, and that is a very difficult effect to achieve.' So much of the atmosphere of *Little Dorrit* is created by de Keyser's impressive versatility of technique. He employs his formidable skill across a whole range of sets, from gloomy interiors, where it is easy to believe that the characters really are lit only by candles or the flat dim light of a north-facing window, to brightly lit society scenes where everything is bathed in gold.

Vidgeon also is a master. He came up the hard way, twenty-five years a focus puller, mostly for that truly great British cinematographer Douglas Slocombe.[22] In Vidgeon's hands, 'The film seems to shine with light like the glow of an oil painting,' wrote Nigella Lawson in the *Sunday Times*. This is because he uses a lot of direct lighting which intensifies the colour and, incidentally, gives him a considerable degree of sharpness foreground to back. Vidgeon describes his time at Sands as 'the happiest I've spent on a set,'[23] adding – as a joke – that he'd like to send Edzard off 'to do an episode of *Miami Vice* so she sees how other people do it.'[24]

Photograph 41
Ron Emslie and Simon Slater, burlesque players in *The Fool*

Striving for excellence

Two great performances: Charlie Sutton the industrial chimney sweep – whose story I was not able to tell for TV back in my Granada days (p. 34) – doing Shakespeare's Polonius; and Miriam Margolyes as Flora Finching, the tall 'lily' of a child who grows up to be a 'chattering peony, broad and short of breath, diffuse and silly', in Edzard's *Little Dorrit*. Charlie's performance, impromptu and very well-oiled, was given to passers-by at midnight on the pavement outside his house. Miriam's was professional, inspired, wonderfully comic and technically perfect.

Shortly after we finished on *The Fool*, I bumped into Margolyes at Oxford Circus. Her immensely successful one-woman show, *Dickens' Women*, was about to move to the West End and she was getting a lot of offers from America. I couldn't help feeling how sad it is that so few British producers have been able to capitalise on her talent – but that's the British film industry for you. Yet there *is* some hope, just a glimmer. In the UK today £100m worth of cinema tickets are sold every year, more than twice the number sold just six years ago and that's got to mean something, hasn't it? The trouble is that less than five per cent of the films shown in our cinemas are made here. In France, where the industry is subsidised, 125 cinema features are made every year. In Britain we are lucky if we complete a third of that number. Oh yes, the cinema is alive and well in Britain. It is just film-making that's on its knees.

So why is it that so few of our films make money? Some would say that British film-making is bedevilled by nepotism and ignorance; half the people in it being toffee-nosed college kids, their minds full of film theory and (God forbid) semiotics, the other half being hairy-backed morons who, when they hear the first lot discussing *film noir*, think someone is planning a night shoot. This is not my view. I think, quite simply, that we've run out of stories. While Americans tell stories about deities and super-beings intervening in the lives of men (*Star Wars*, *Terminator*, *Ghost Busters* etc.) we Brits seem incapable of escaping our literary heritage.

As Charlie Sutton – quoting Charles Kingsley – said as he took off his hat to yet another industrial boiler driving by on its way to the scrapyard: 'Is it progress we have to report?'

Photograph 42
Miriam Margolyes in *The Fool*

Endings

A snow job at Christmas

Christmas 1988. Over the Scottish borders Pan Am flight 103 fell out of the sky exploded by a terrorist bomb. In Armenia an earthquake meant that President Gorbachev had to rush home from the US cancelling a planned visit to London. On the M1 another aeroplane crashed on approach to East Midlands airport and then, on Boxing Day, Richard, my father-in-law, died.

And all the while a publisher's publicist was trying to get me into Number Ten, Downing Street to shoot some exclusive pictures for a book[25] to be published on the tenth anniversary of Mrs Thatcher's accession to power. As quickly as windows opened in the Prime Minister's diary, they were closed in mine and vice versa.

Have you ever tried to arrange a funeral over Christmas?

There was a film biography that Richard had always liked about the pianist Liberace, though I don't think it meant anything to him that the director was Tony Palmer. Why should it?

At the hospital the ward sister had a seasonal twist of tinsel in her hair. While we paid our last respects my six-year-old-son – a noble creature – took control of the situation, addressing her formally, with his hands behind his back, thanking her for looking after his grandad. The funeral took place on New Year's Eve and we three sons-in-law (it would be difficult to imagine a team of pall-bearers which was less well-matched physically) somehow managed to carry the coffin without causing embarrassment. (Bent in half, I took consolation from the thought that it would have been a deal worse had a fourth, rather short, son-in-law made it from Australia.) The funeral director was called B. Sweet.

My trip to Number Ten eventually took place on Twelfth Night. When I went in there was a Christmas tree on the pavement by the door; when I came out it had gone. Dead on time, freshly coiffured and powdered, vibrant in Tory blue, more eager than any film star, Mrs Thatcher was at my elbow.

'I find it never works,' she said fixing me with a glare, 'unless I am staring at the camera.'

She held no candle for spontaneity. *So* much control, so *little* left to chance! I was glad only that I had kept the foreign rights to the pictures. That way there was, at least, a chance that I might avoid the session turning into a snow job.

Photograph 43
'Margaret Thatcher looks stunning yes,
But why no nipples in the *Daily Express*?'
John Cooper Clarke[26]

30 APRIL 1989

SUNDAY EXPRESS
magazine

10
YEARS AT
No 10
DIARY OF A DECADE

Poor Mr Gorbachev

Together we made our gradual progress through the gilt fripperies of state and pre-negotiated set-ups. On the stairs in front of a portrait of Anthony Eden, her palms upturned as though she expected something else to fall out of the sky, Mrs Thatcher indicated the fresh red decor and said:

'Just for Mr Gorbachev. Poor Mr Gorbachev.' And then: 'Well, take another one, won't you? What if I blinked?'

Inside her office, all beige carpet and Bromley loungeware, the loose covers and the cream curtains crawled with a pattern of red flowers and green leaves. A horrible John Piper, all in blue, guarded the doorway.

'Absolutely no pictures of the windows!' a press secretary hissed in my ear. (I wasn't to give away vantage points for snipers, it seemed – not that I could see anything through the heavy white netting.)

A golden eagle in bronze, quite out of its tree, stood on a mahogany table behind the sofa. The Prime Minister fussed, adjusting this, plumping that and declined to sit in a green chair which clashed with her vibrant blue.

Five days later we did it all over again at her office in the Palace of Westminster, a large rectangular room with huge mirrors, all Pugin except that at one end a wall had been taken down to reveal an annexe where suburban sofas sat on a carpet under a portrait of Admiral Nelson.

'Harold did that,' said the Prime Minister.

A pinstripe piped up: 'It's where he kept Marcia,' and how we nervous ones did laugh!

Not her, though. Our noise was her cue to press on.

Ministers of state were waiting.

So exit and fast forward four months.

Up on the news stands my picture of Mrs T. smiles down but I'm not smiling back. I'm busy worming out of another invitation – this time to photograph Prince Charles.

You see, Mr B. Sweet has been busy again.

My mother wouldn't have approved of me dodging a royal appointment to attend her funeral, but funerals aren't for the dead, are they? They're for the living and, after all, a chap has only one mother.

Anyway there are too many royals these days, wouldn't you say?

Photograph 44
Hugh Lloyd in *The Fool*

Photograph 45
The curtain call: Norah Connolly, Ron Emslie, Simon Slater, Miranda Richardson, Michael Feast, Knight Mantell, John Moore, Joanne Brookes in *The Fool*

Photograph 46
Not a movie still, just an appreciative Bank Holiday audience at an open-air brass band concert in Barnoldswick, Lancashire

Notes

1 *In Our Own Image*, Fred Ritchin (Aperture, 1990).

2 *On Photography*, Susan Sontag (Penguin, 1979), pp. 17-18.

3 *Unknown Pleasures* (Fact 10) and *Closer* (Fact XXV), albums by Joy Division.

4 'Magnum Photos, Inc., a cooperative agency founded in 1947 by Henri Cartier-Bresson, Robert Capa, Maria Eisner, David Seymour (Chim), George Rodger, and William and Rita Vandivert, and today considered the world's most renowned collective of photographers.' *In Our Time* by William Manchester (André Deutsch, 1989).

5 See *Masters of Starlight* by David Fahey and Linda Rich (Columbus Books, 1988), p. 222.

6 *The Decisive Moment* by Henri Cartier-Bresson (Simon and Schuster, 1952).

7 Interview by Michael Hallett published in the *British Journal of Photography*, 13 December 1990.

8 BTEC Higher National Diploma in Documentary Photography as taught at Gwent College of Higher Education, Newport, Wales.

9 *Winogrand* by John Szarkowski, Museum of Modern Art, New York, 1988.

10 *A Time There Was*.

11 *At The Haunted End of the Day*.

12 John Preston, *The Times*, 24 May 1984.

13 Elizabeth Dunn, *7 Days*, *Sunday Telegraph*, 15 April 1990.

14 Ibid.

15 *Julian Bream – A Life on the Road* by Tony Palmer with photographs by Daniel Meadows (Macdonald, 1982).

16 The official 100th birthday portrait of Stravinsky, which won the Special Jury Prize at the San Francisco Film and Television Festival (1982).

17 Storaro won Oscars for his photography on Coppola's *Apocalypse Now* (1979), Beatty's *Reds* (1982) and Bertolucci's *The Last Emperor* (1988).

18 *Mozart in Japan*.

19 *Little Dorrit* is in fact two separate films which tell the same story but from different points of view.

20 As described in the article 'Lateral Projection for Little Dorrit' in *American Cinematographer*, vol. 69 no.1, January 1988, p. 62.

21 *Sunday in the Country* (1984) directed by Bertrand Tavernier.

22 Douglas Slocombe, British cinematographer of, among many others, the following films: *Kind Hearts and Coronets* (1949), *The Lavender Hill Mob* (1951), *The Servant* (1963), *The Lion in Winter* (1968), *Raiders of the Lost Ark* (1981), *Never Say Never Again* (1983).

23 *Eastman in Camera*, Kodak house journal, Summer 1990.

24 *Sunday Times*, 29 April 1990.

25 *Ten Years at Number 10* by Roland Flamini, Aurum Press, 1989.

26 From the LP record *Où est la Maison de Fromage?* by John Cooper Clarke, April Music/Spilt Beans, 1978-80.

Some equipment notes

All the pictures in this book were shot on Olympus OM2N and OM1N cameras, but at the time of writing I am going through a crisis because they are all starting to get old and, since they are not made any more, I have had to invest in some very expensive state-of-the-art Nikons.

I am very conservative in my choice of equipment. Once I have found something which suits me I stick with it until it falls apart. I dislike cameras which are heavy – you don't want to stand around for ten hours a day on a film set with a bag full of Nikon F4s – and I have always resisted cameras powered by batteries. Living in the sticks, working in London so much and travelling a lot by public transport, I tend to carry only the minimum amount of equipment I need to do the job. I dislike purpose-built camera bags, first because they shout out to passers-by: 'I'm stuffed with expensive equipment, steal me', and second because they are full of stiffeners and don't collapse when you take things out of them. Instead I have two Hardy fishing bags. Into these fit three Olympus bodies.

Oh, *why* did Olympus give up on the OM-1? It was the quietest 35mm single lens reflex camera ever made and *so* neat.

Two of my Olympuses were fitted with winders, a gadget I use sparingly and then only as a way of advancing the frame so that I don't have to take my eye away from the viewfinder. Alas, both my Nikons (F4 and F-801) come with built-in winders (noisy), neither of which has a manual override – very irritating. I use 24mm, 35mm, 85mm and 180mm lenses of the widest possible apertures, though my favourite lens is still the Zuiko f2 40mm. I don't care much for Nikon's matrix metering system, but the spot metering in the F4 is excellent. Even so, I never expose film without first taking an invercone reading on my old Weston Master V light meter, and even then I always check with the focus puller what stop he has set. The Weston also makes a good pocket calculator for working out the difference between the movie camera's setting at 24 fps, and my own at 1/60 second.

For film I use: Tri-X 400asa for black and white, Ektachrome Tungsten 160asa for artificial light colour, and Fuji 100asa for daylight colour. As I write, a leaflet has just dropped through the letter-box telling me that Kodak is at last going to market a fast (320asa) Tungsten Ektachrome. Hooray!